HIYAAA GUYS !!

THANK YOU SO MUCH
FOR BUYING THIS

I HOPE YOU WILL
ENJOY THIS !! ♡♡

LOVE YA!
@RETNOLARAS

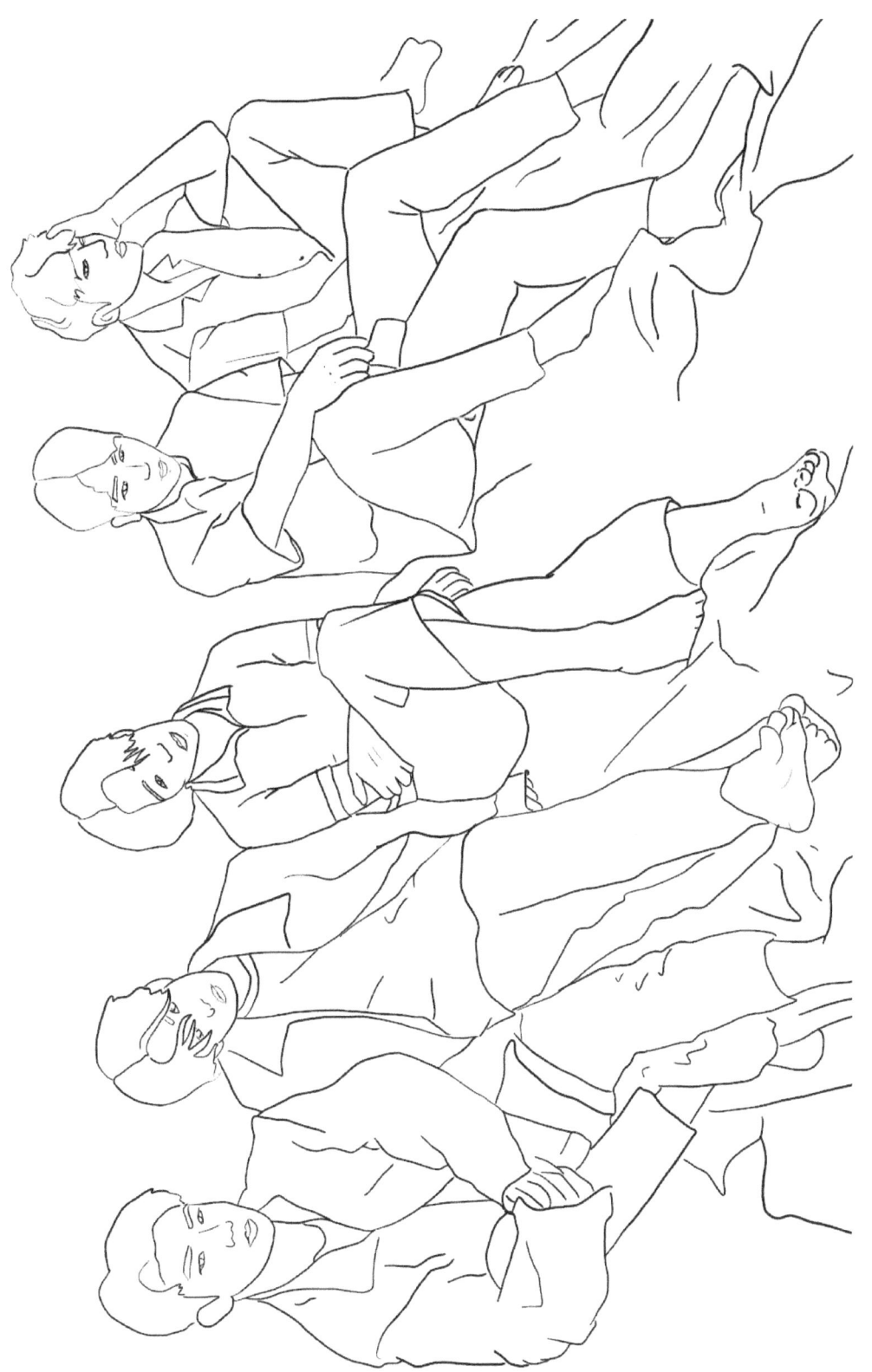

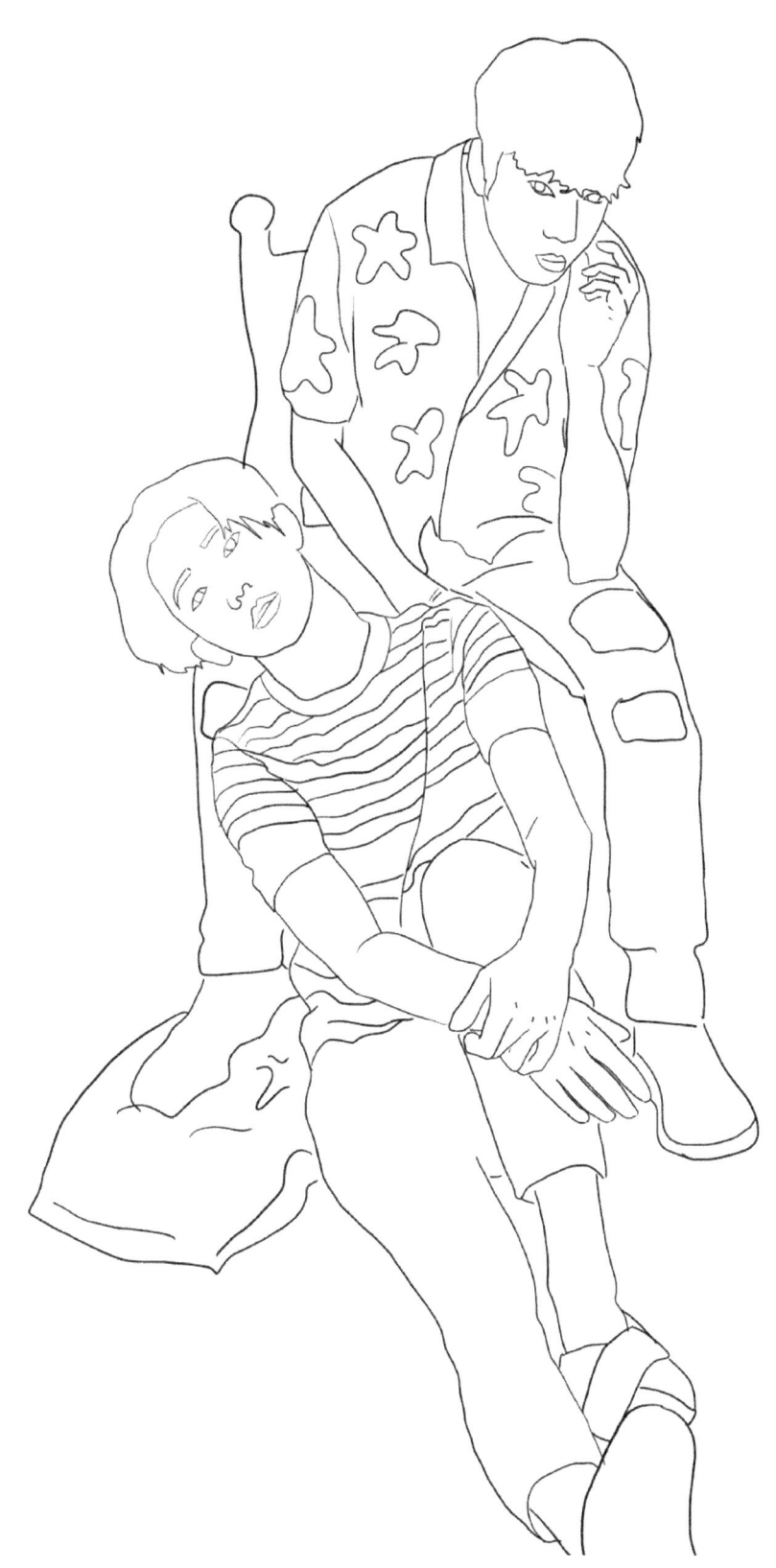

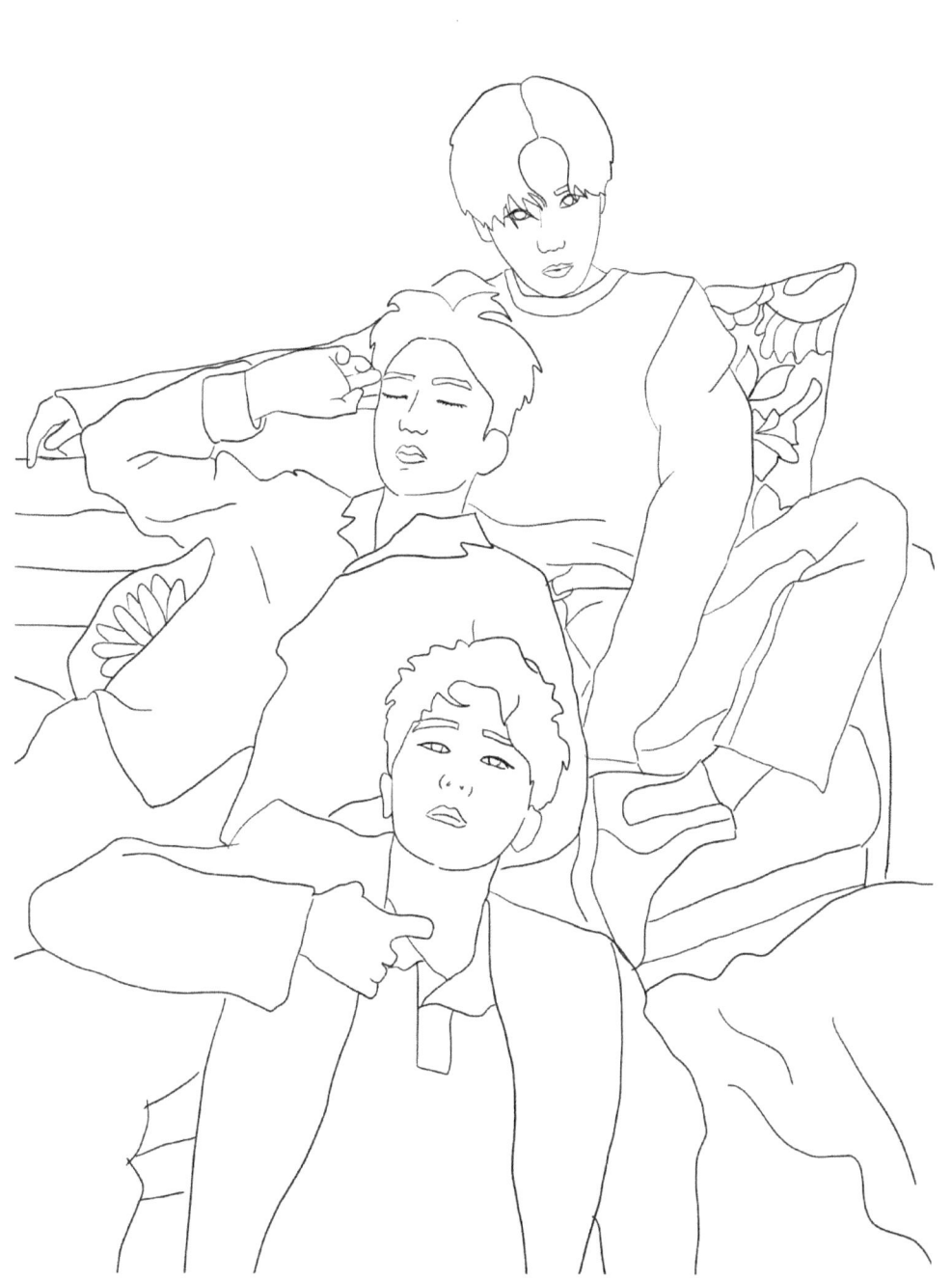

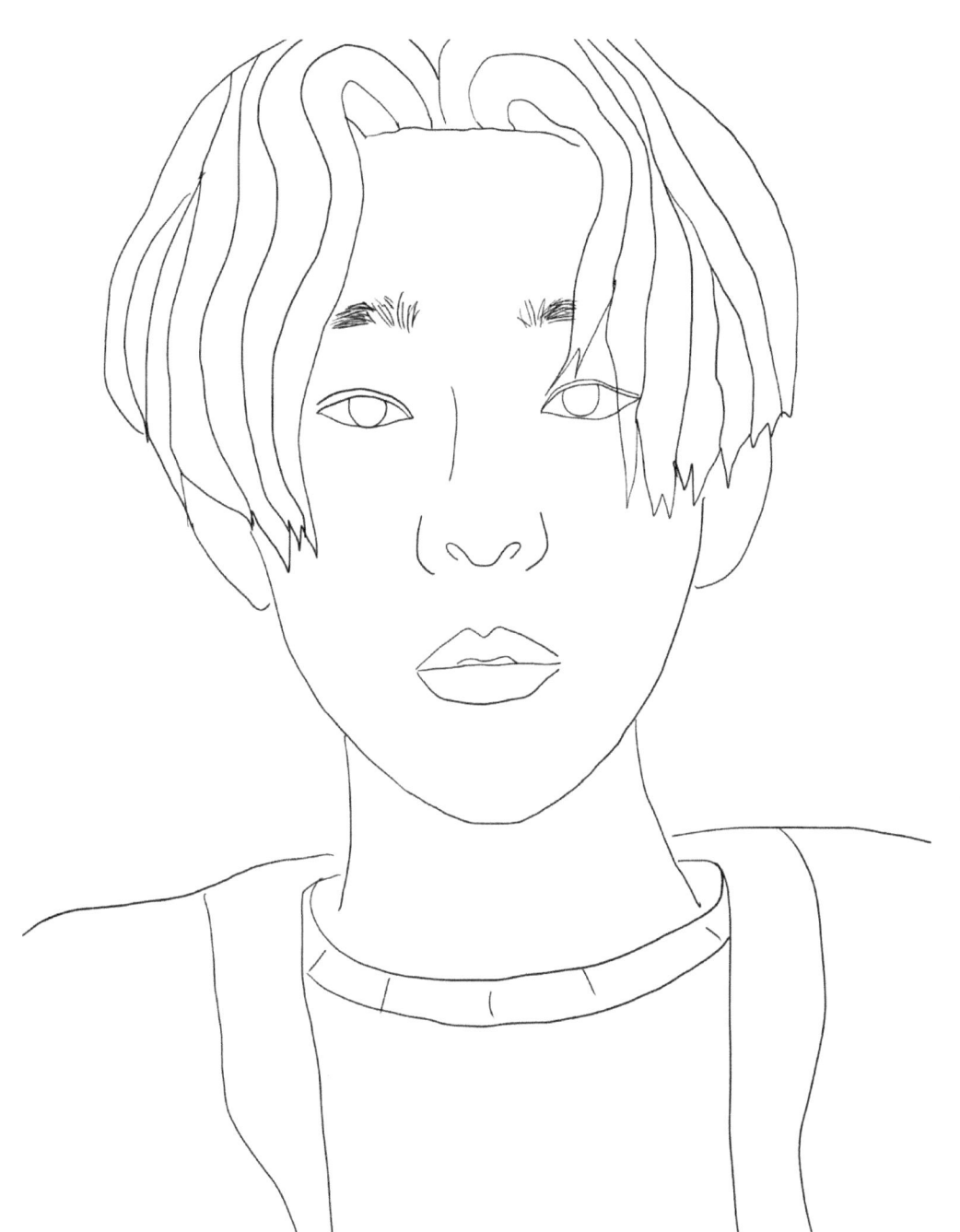

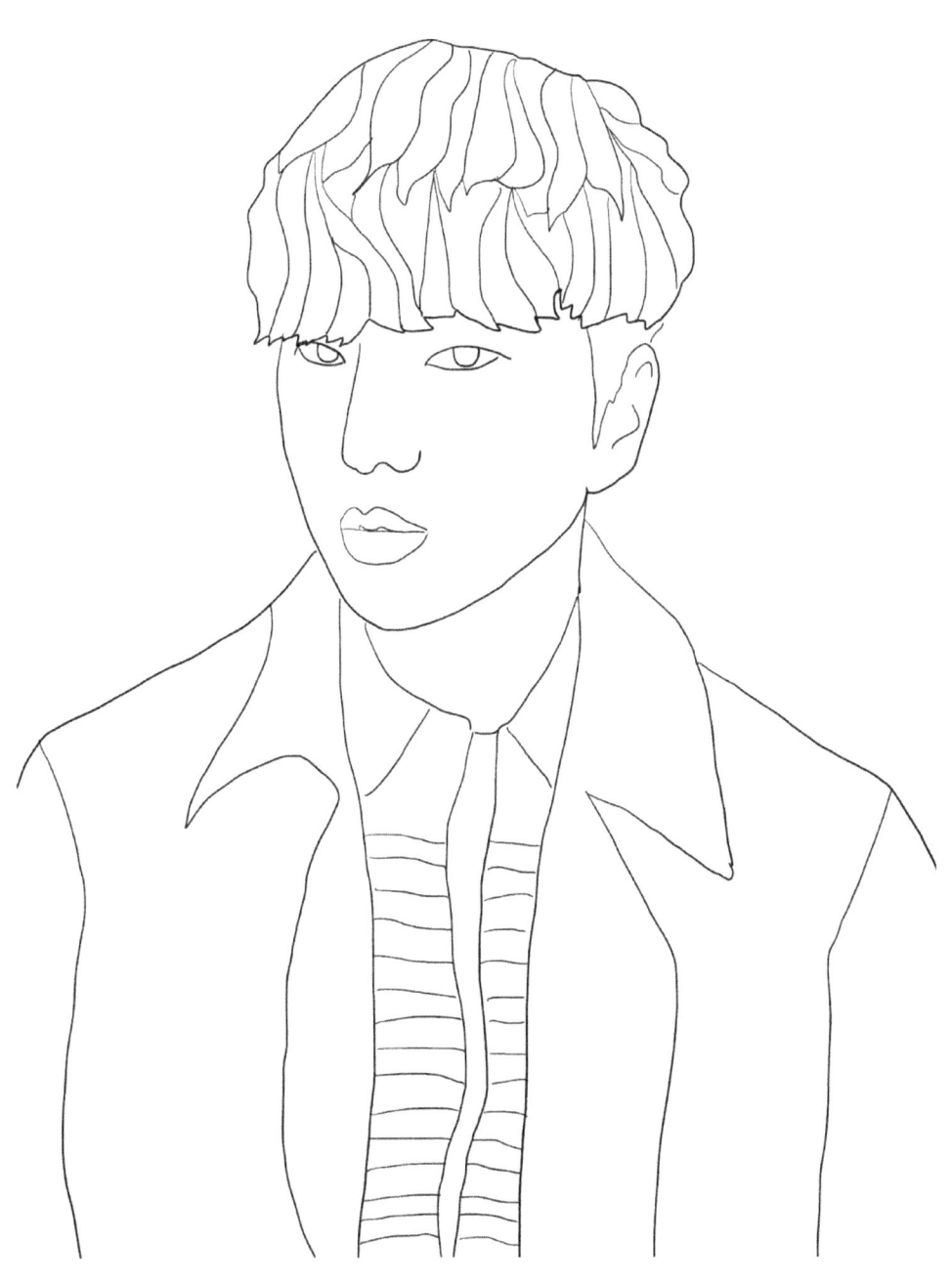

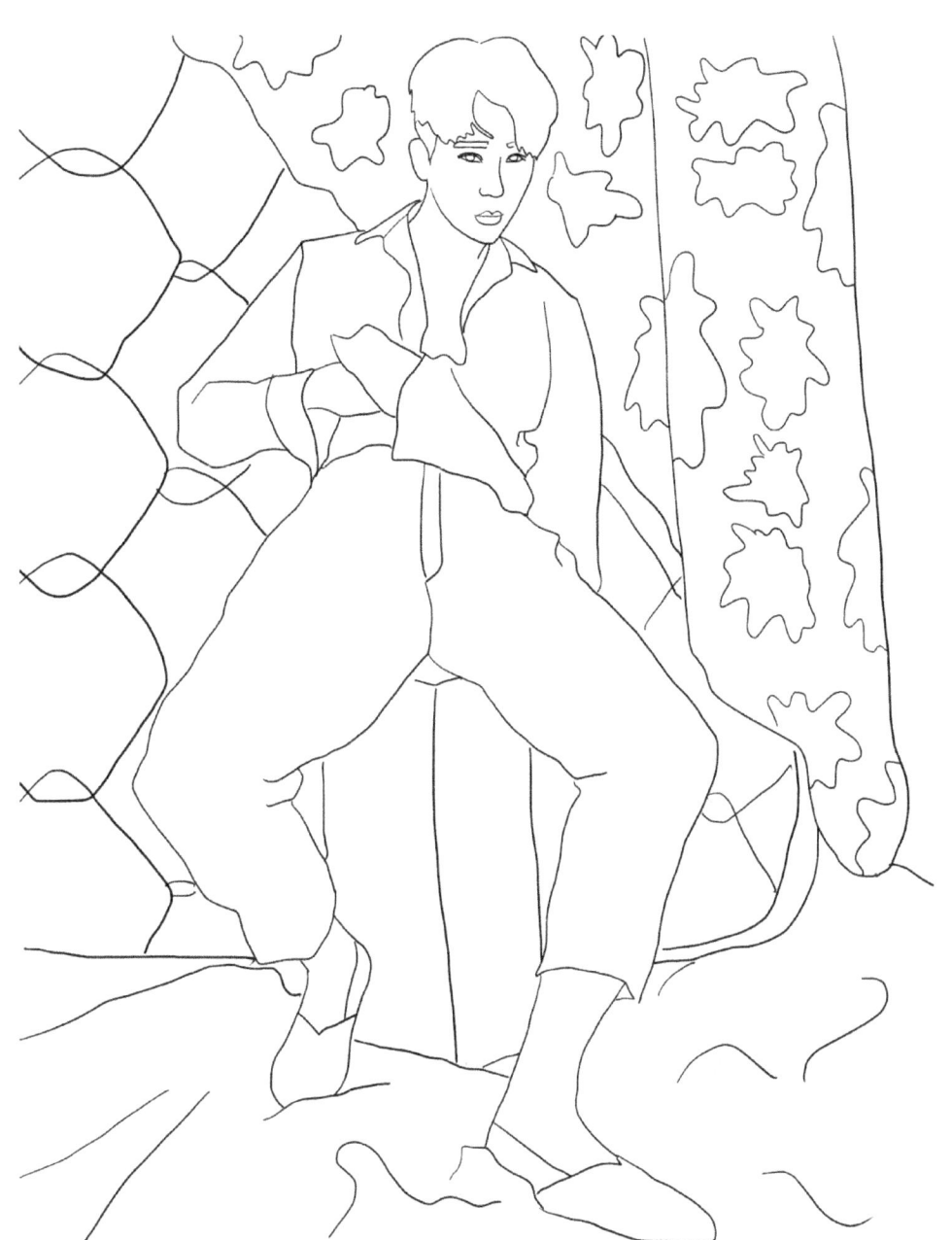

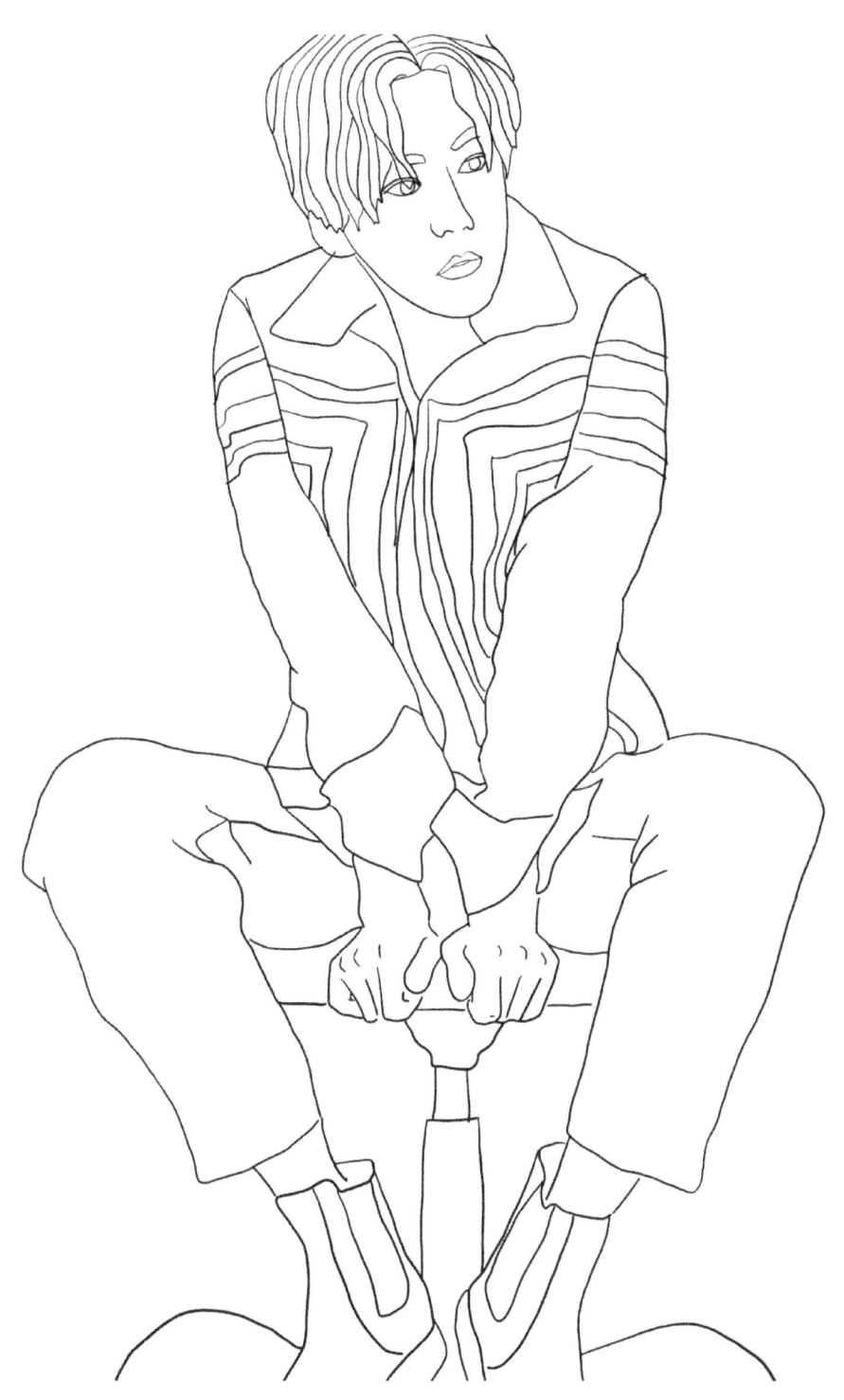

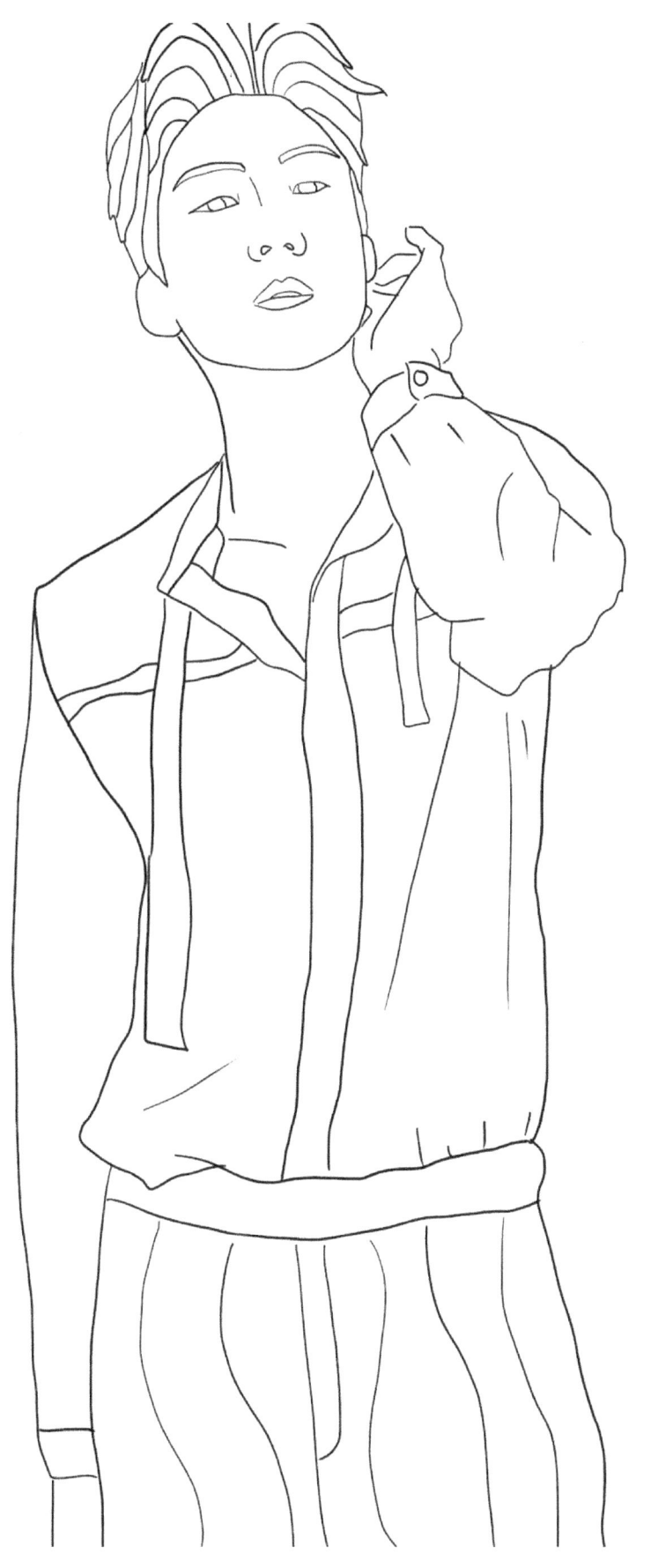

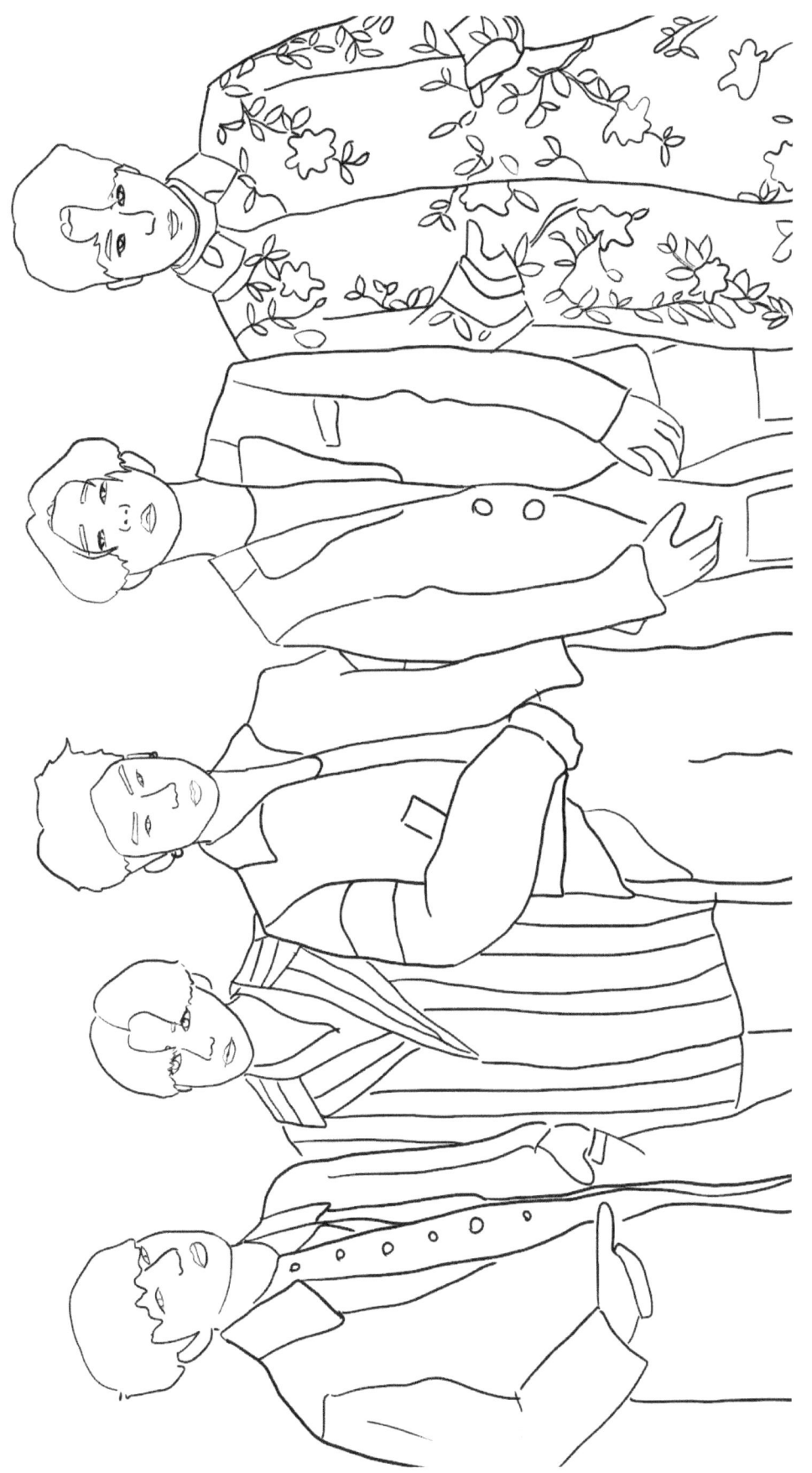

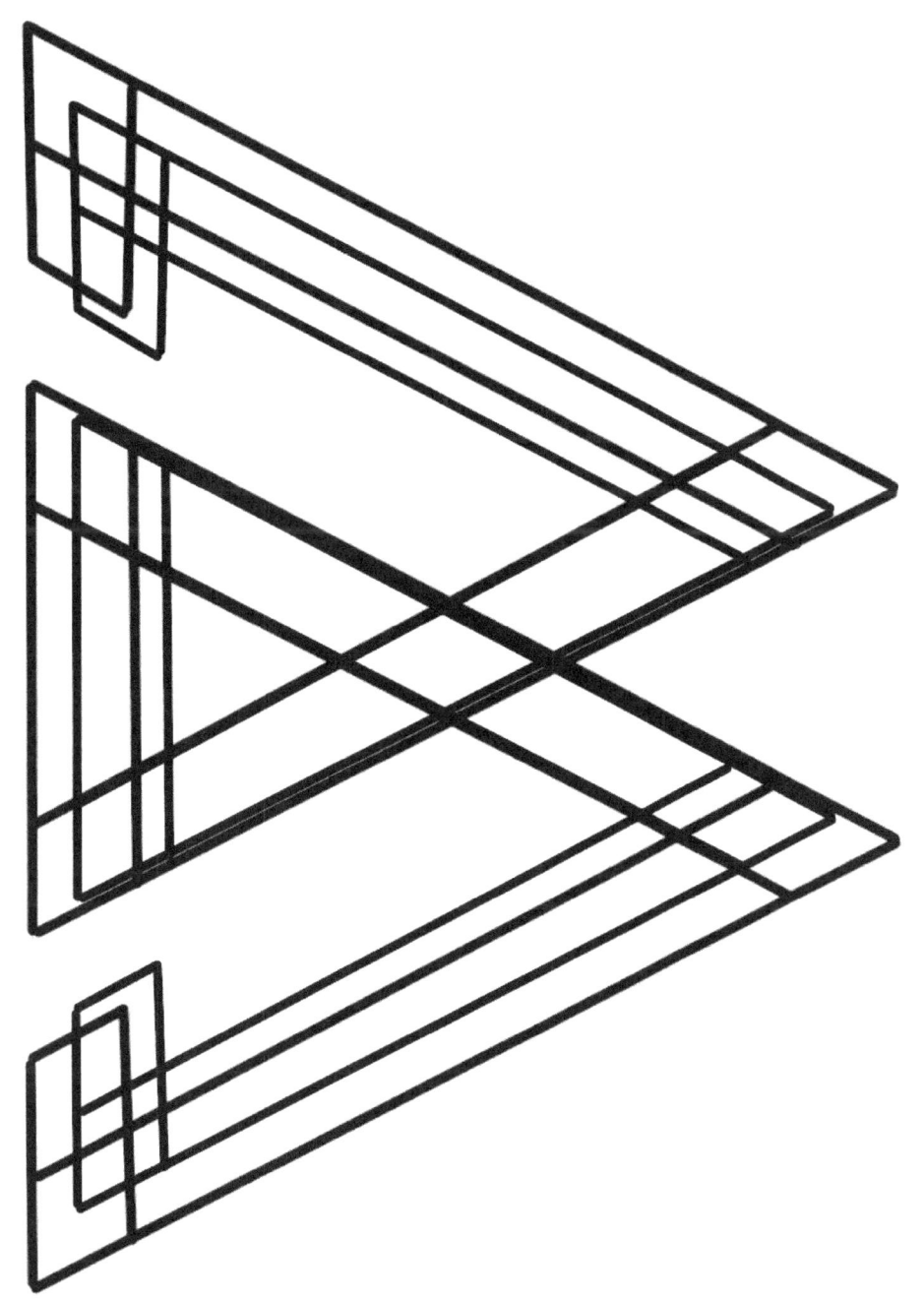

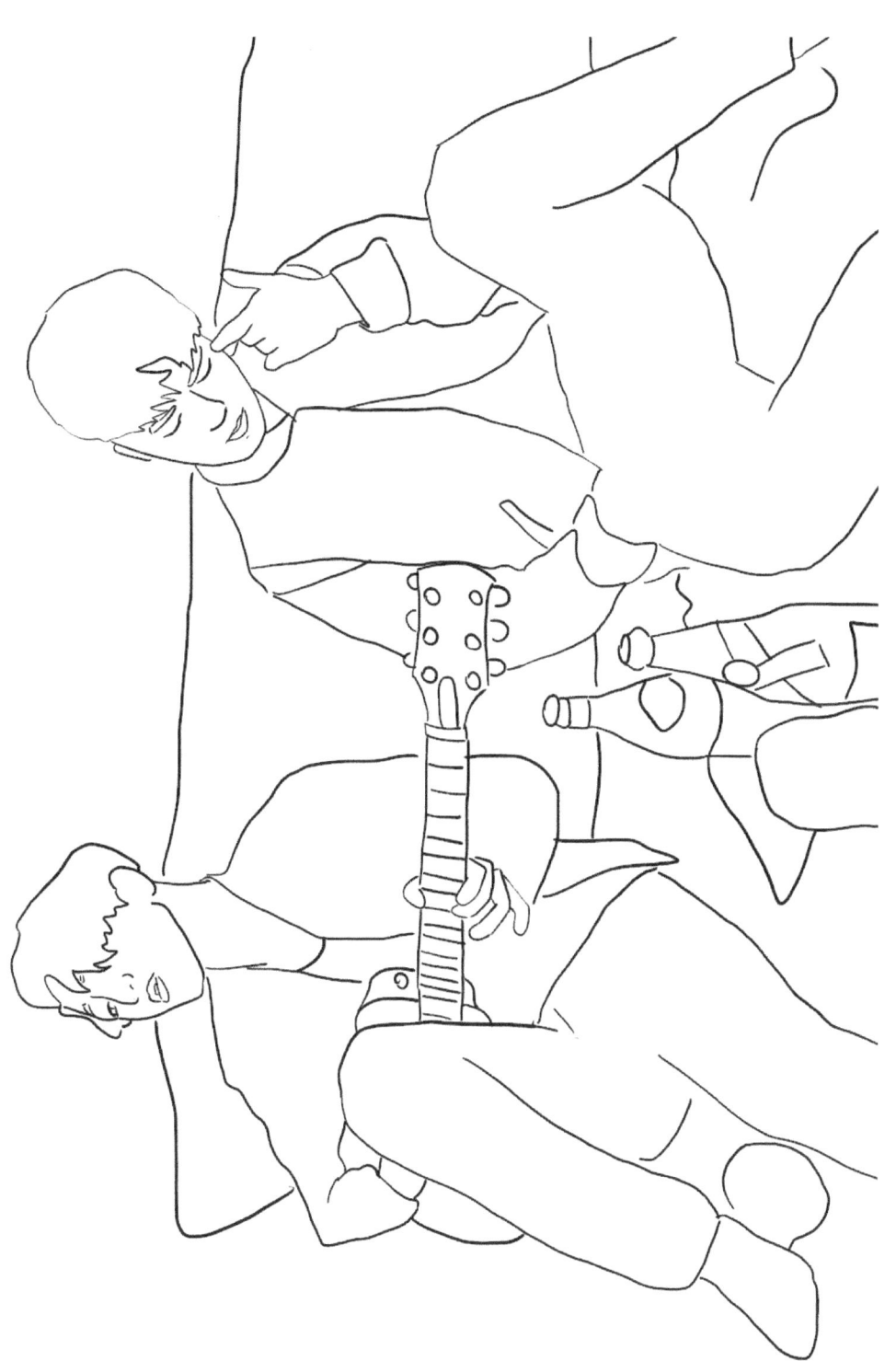

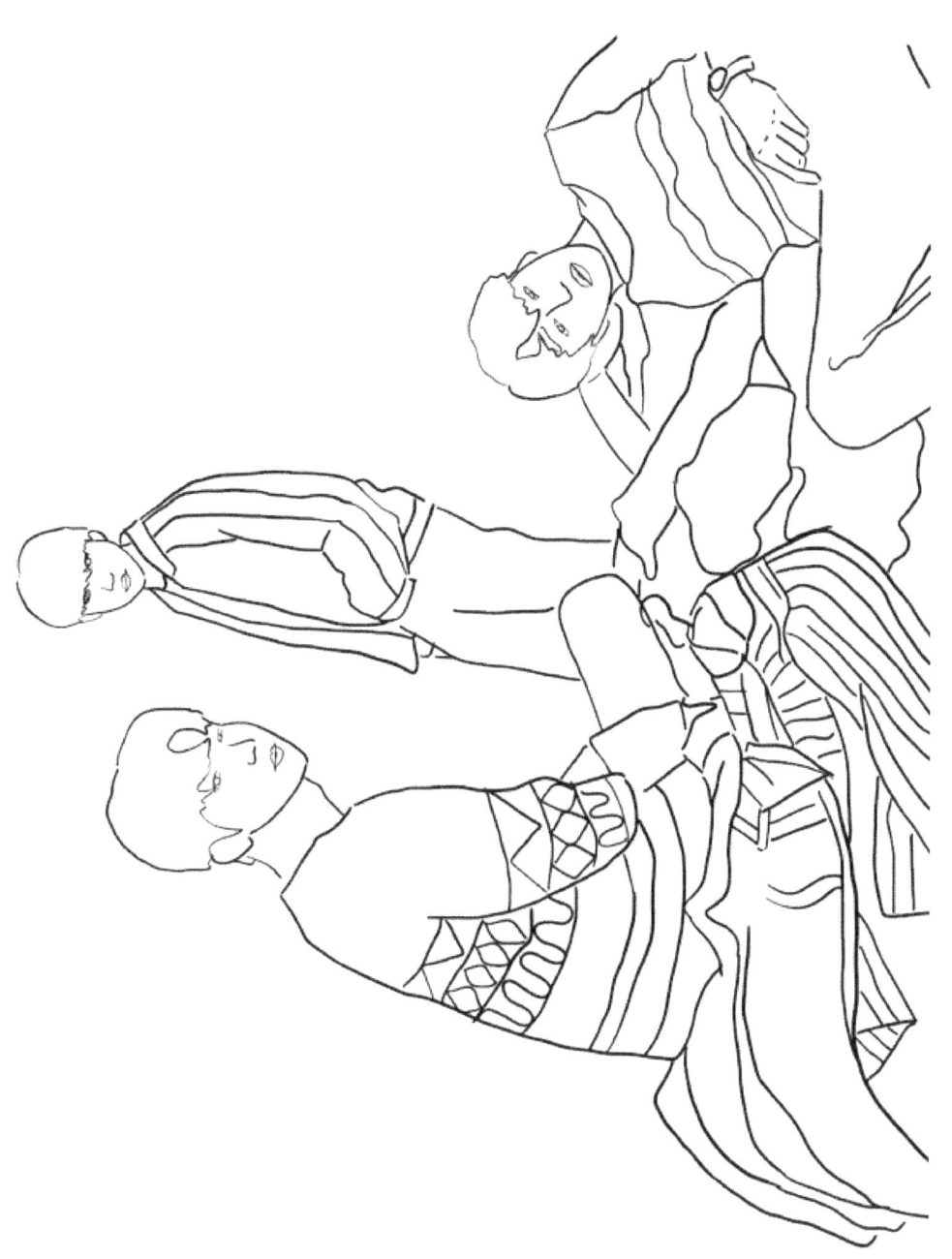

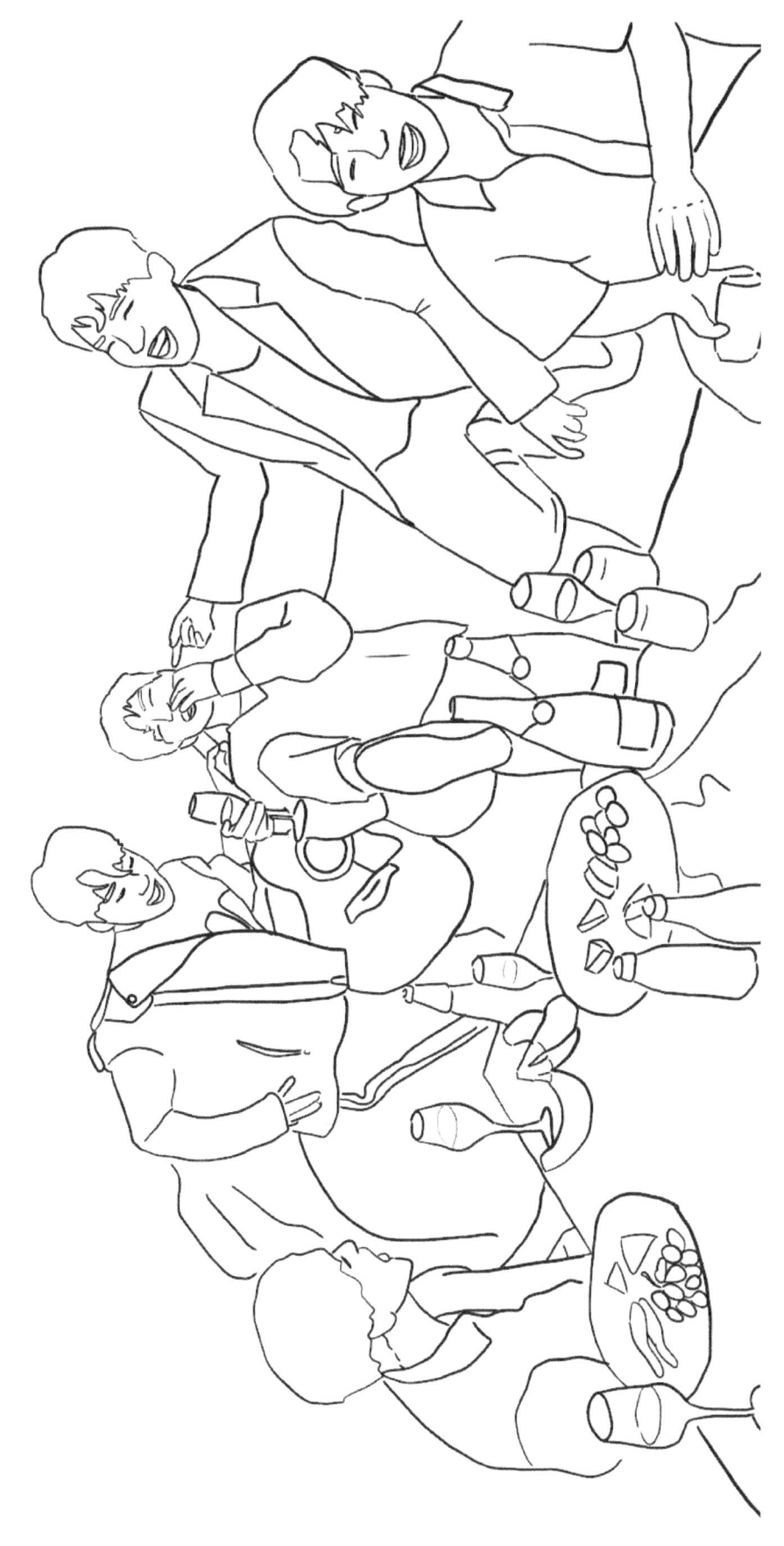

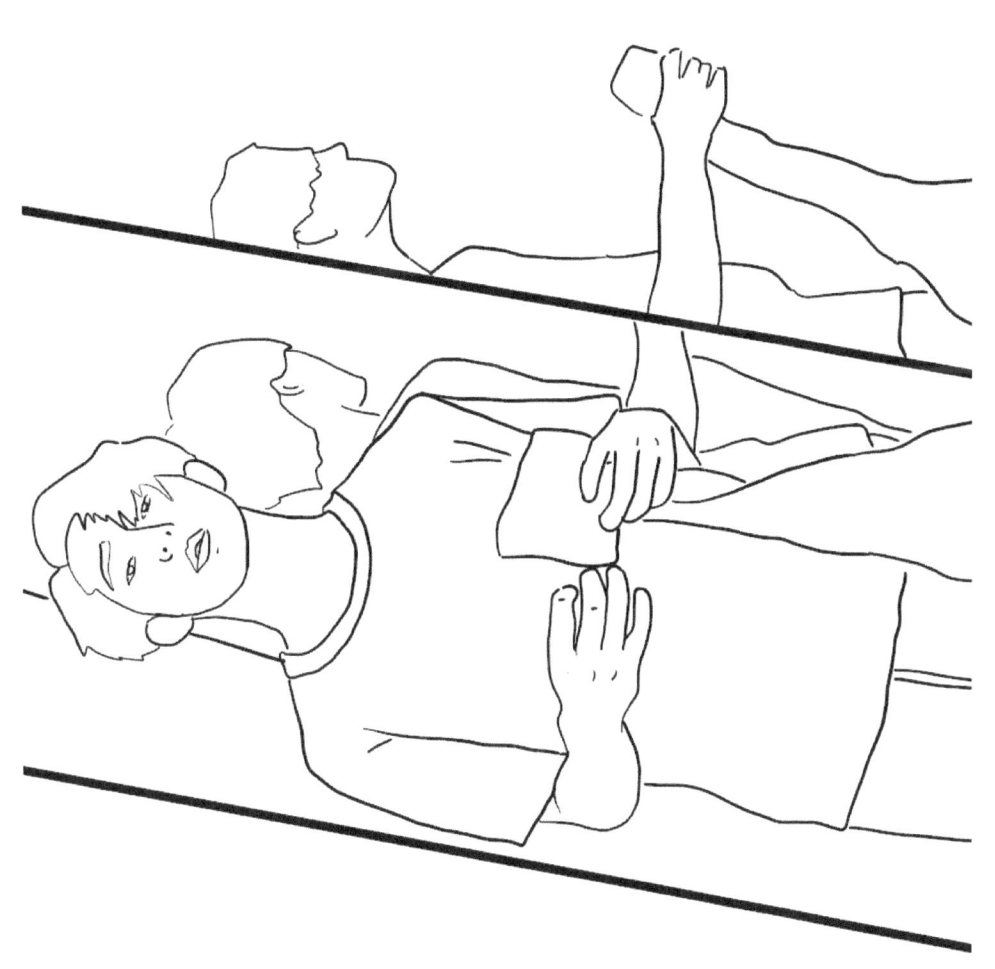

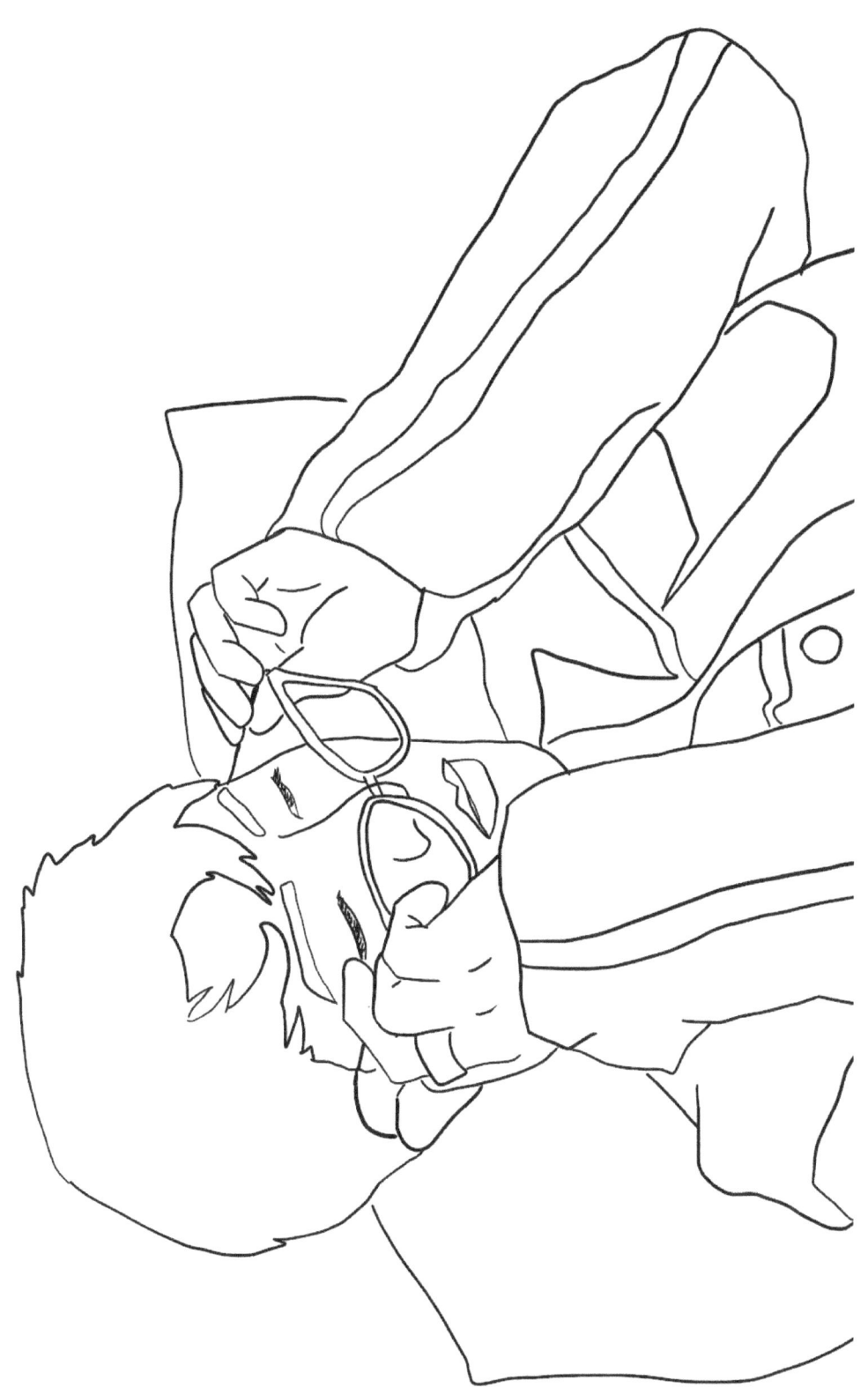

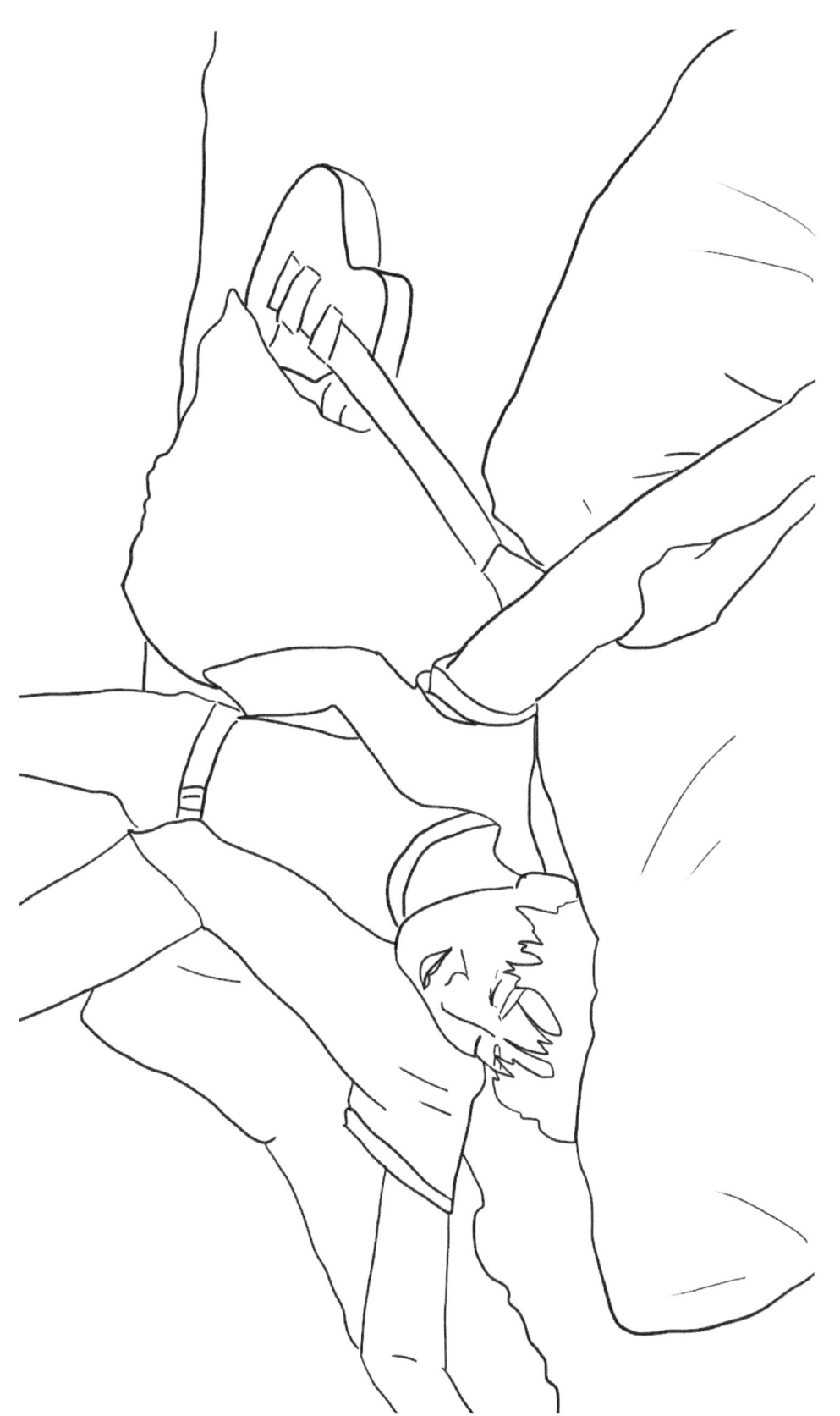

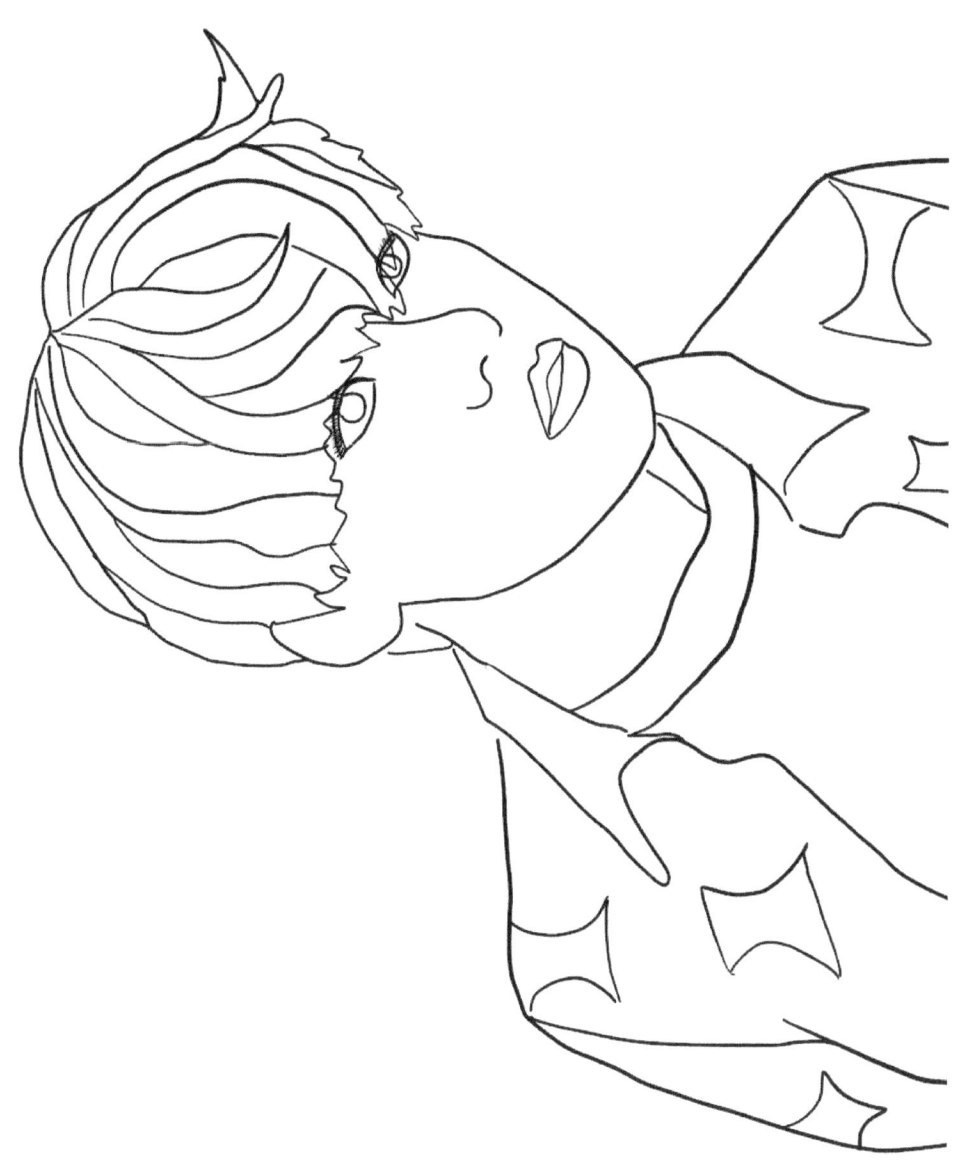

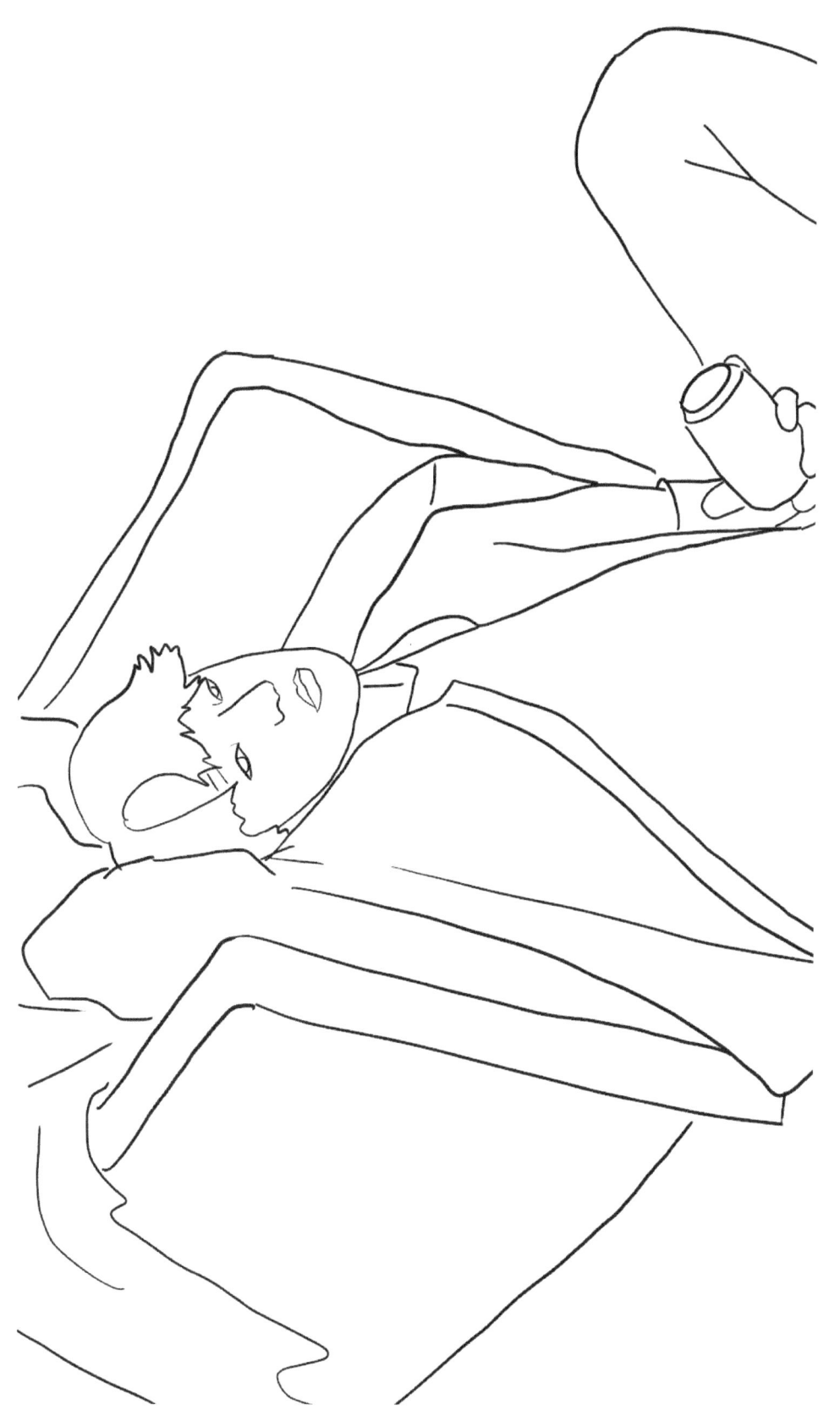

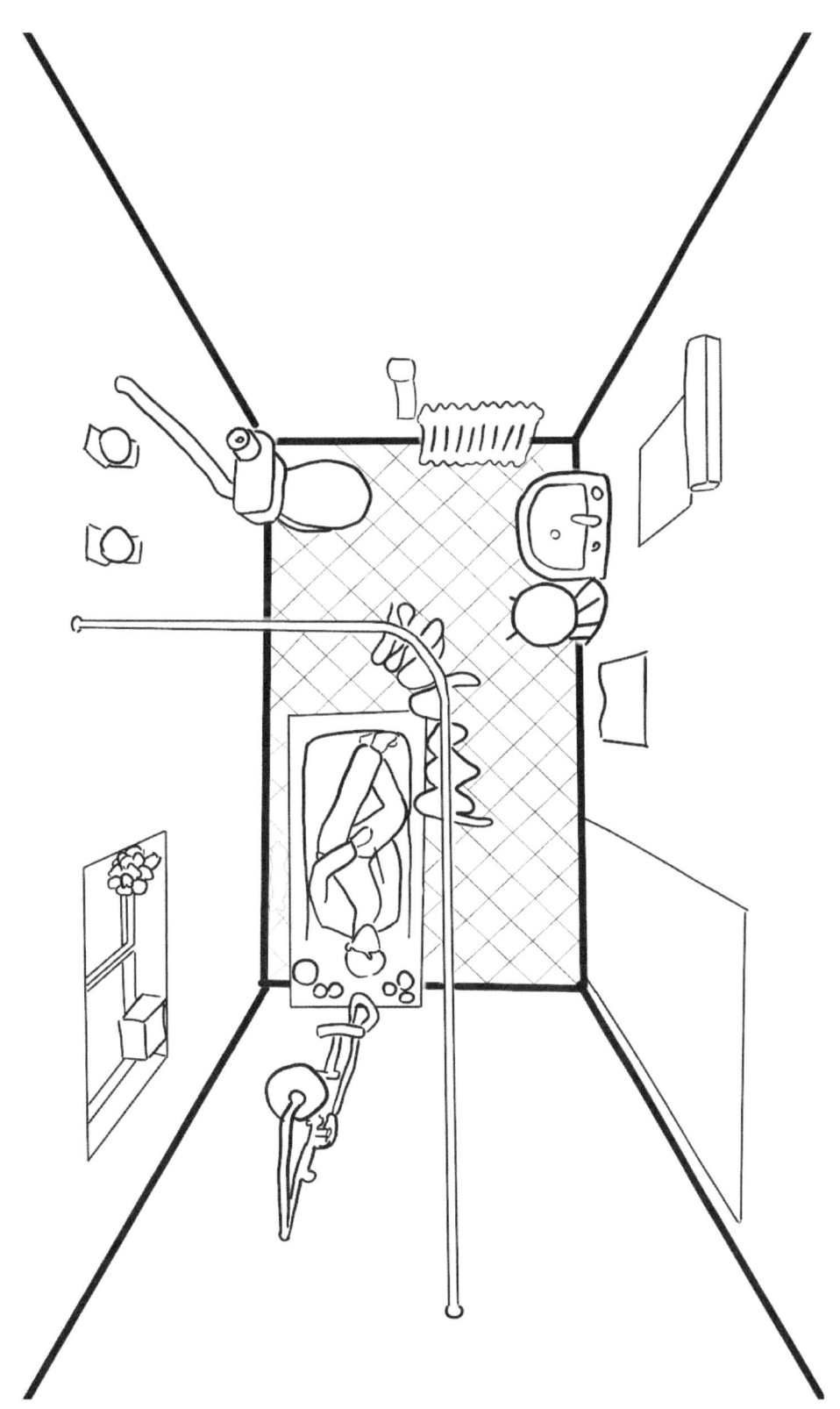

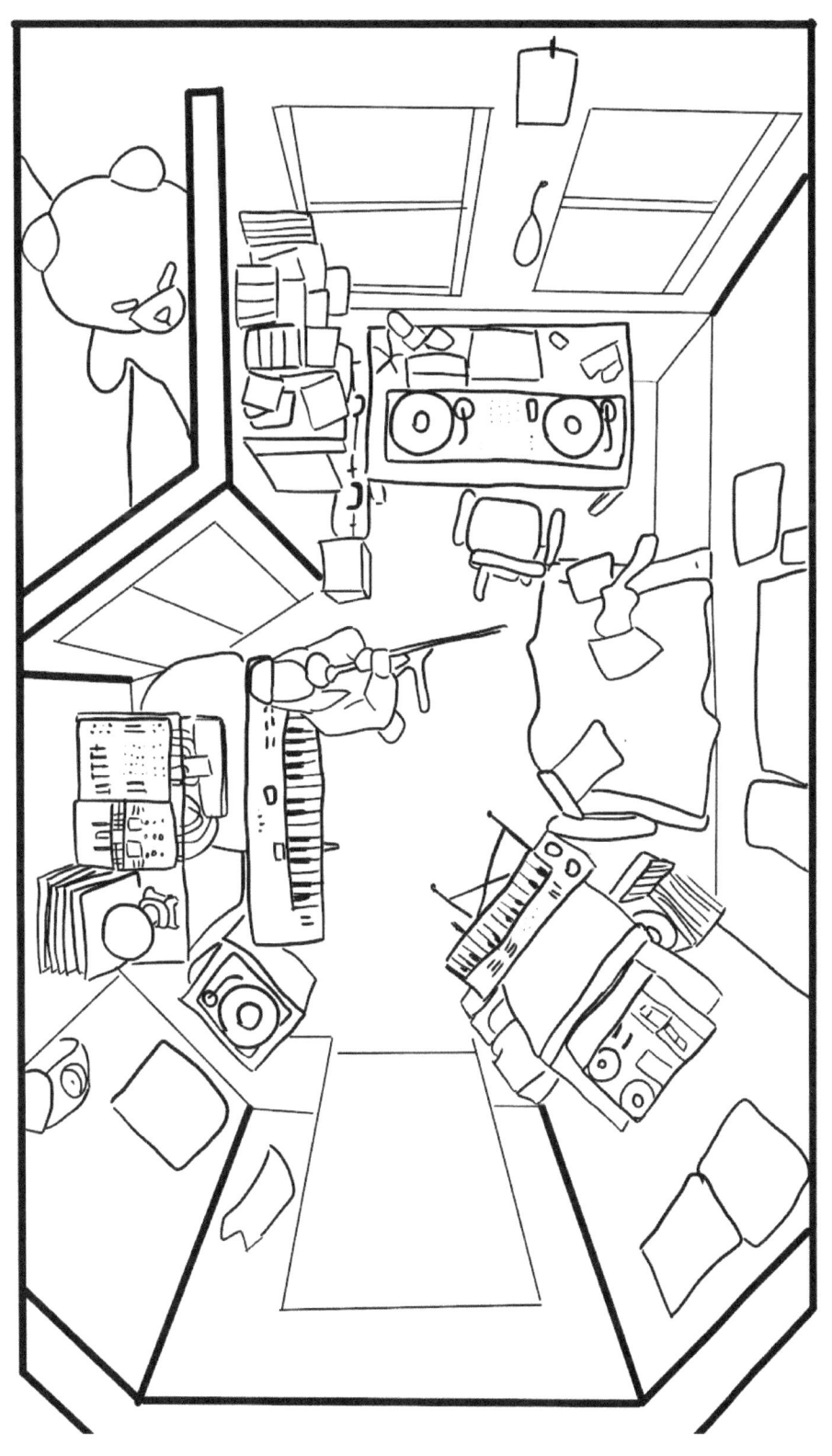

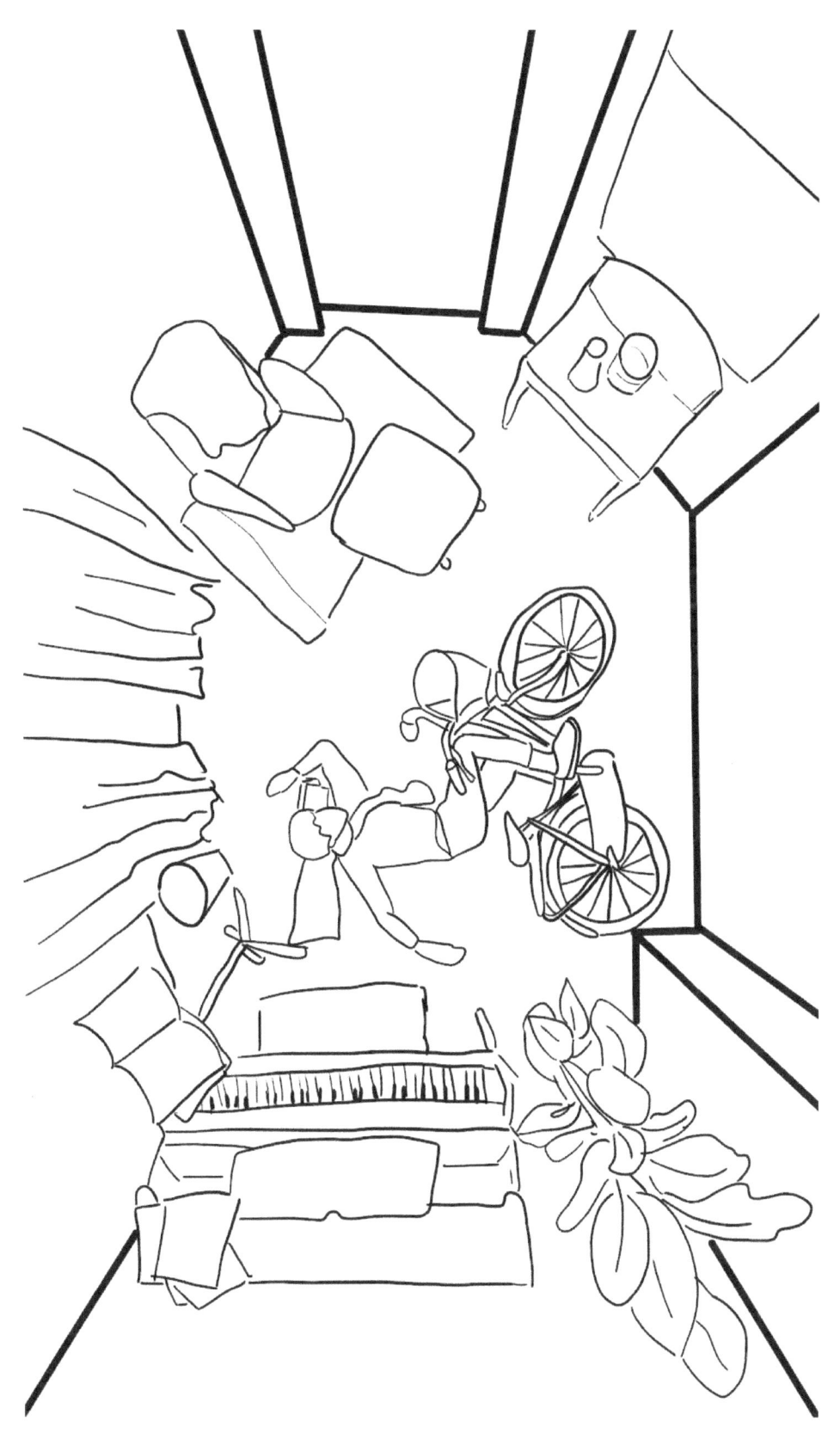

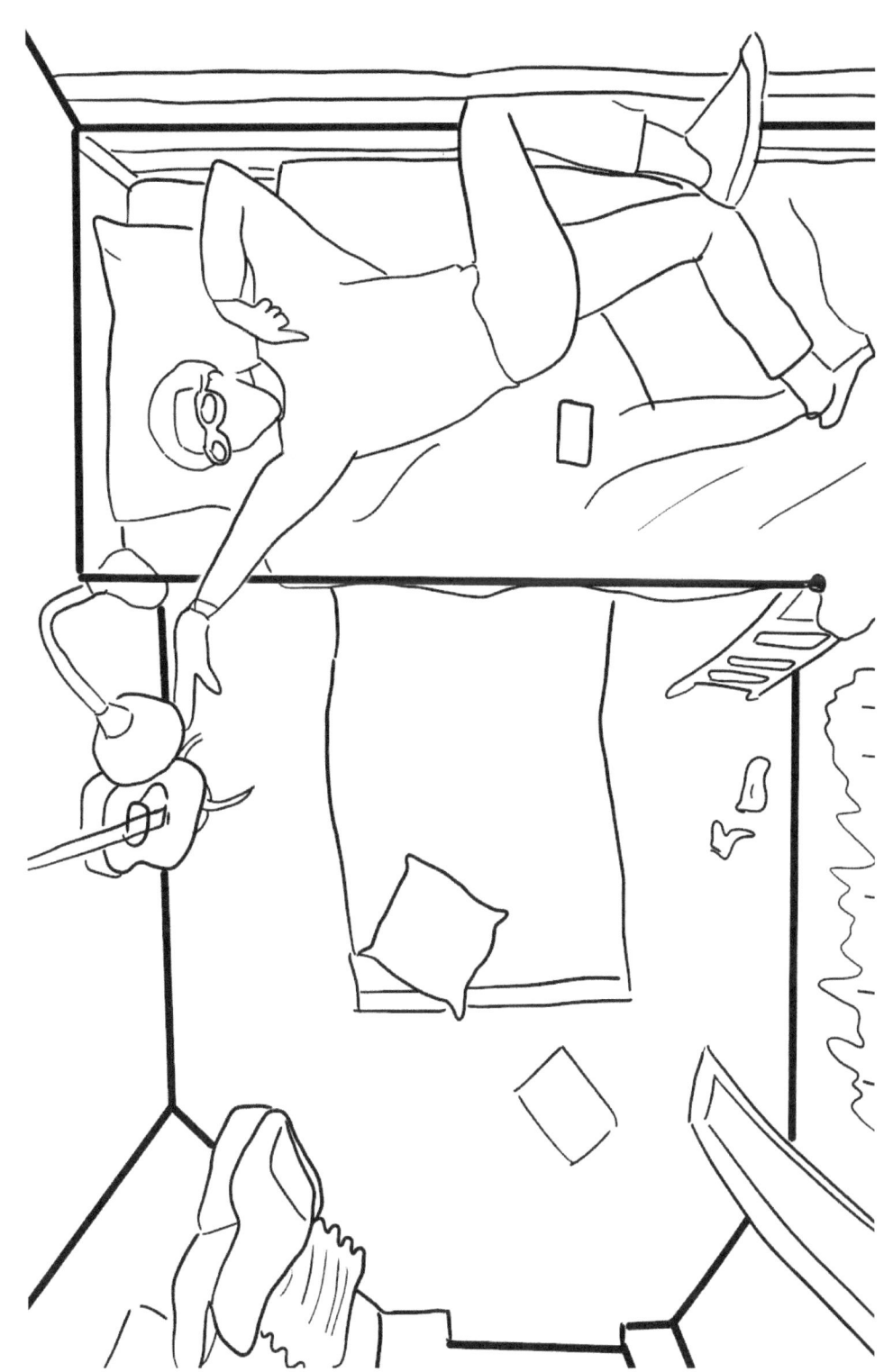

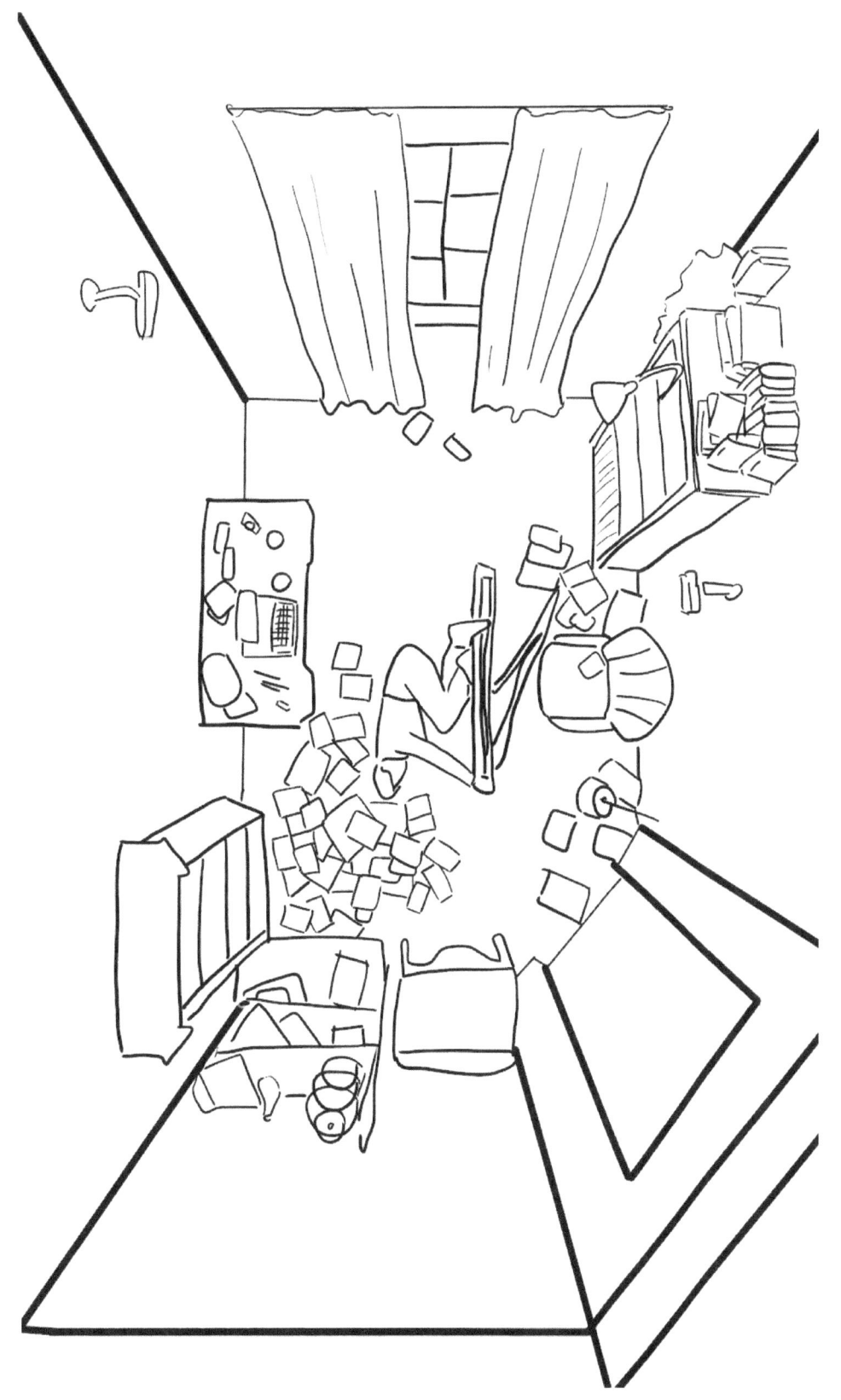

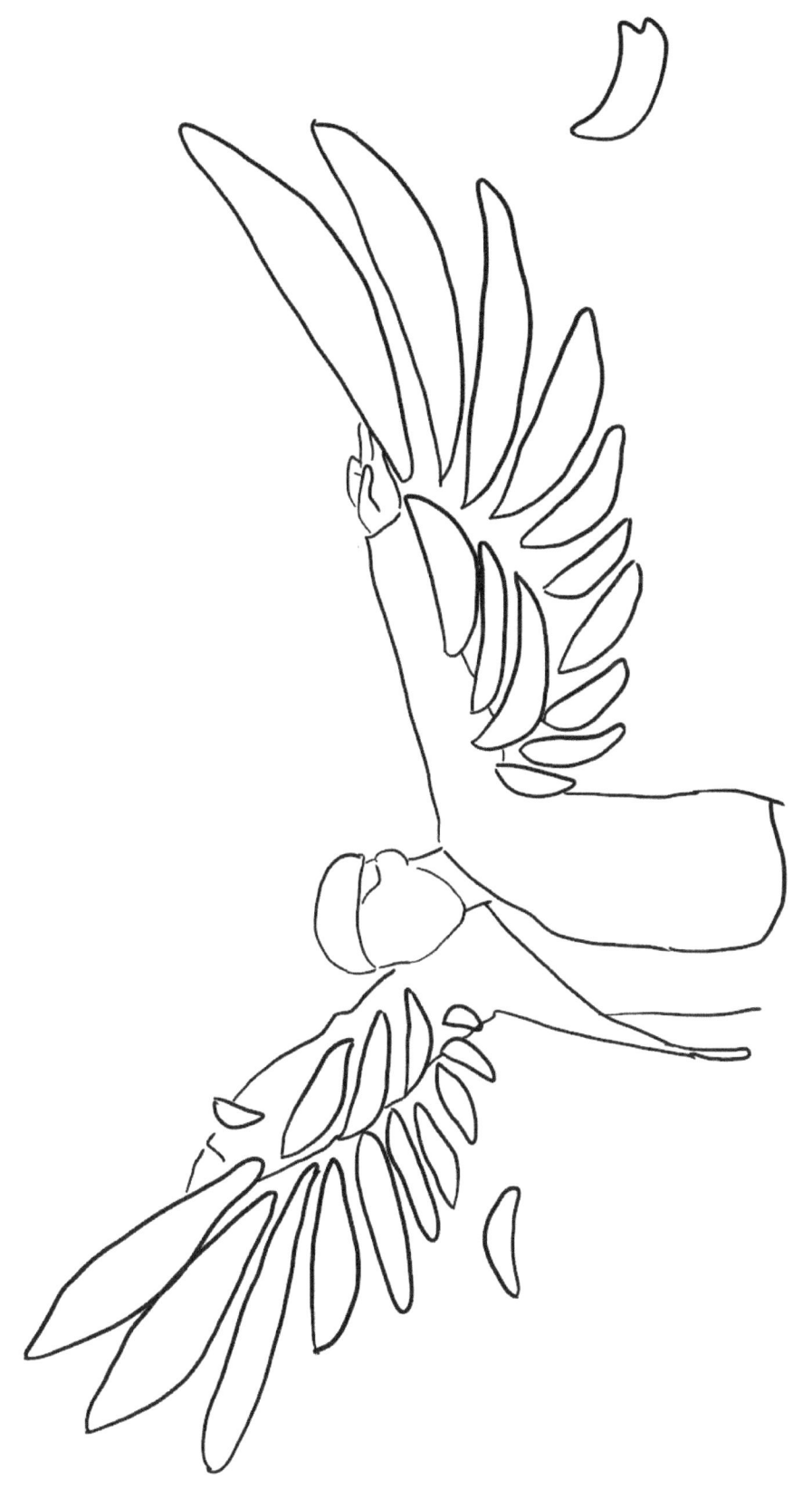

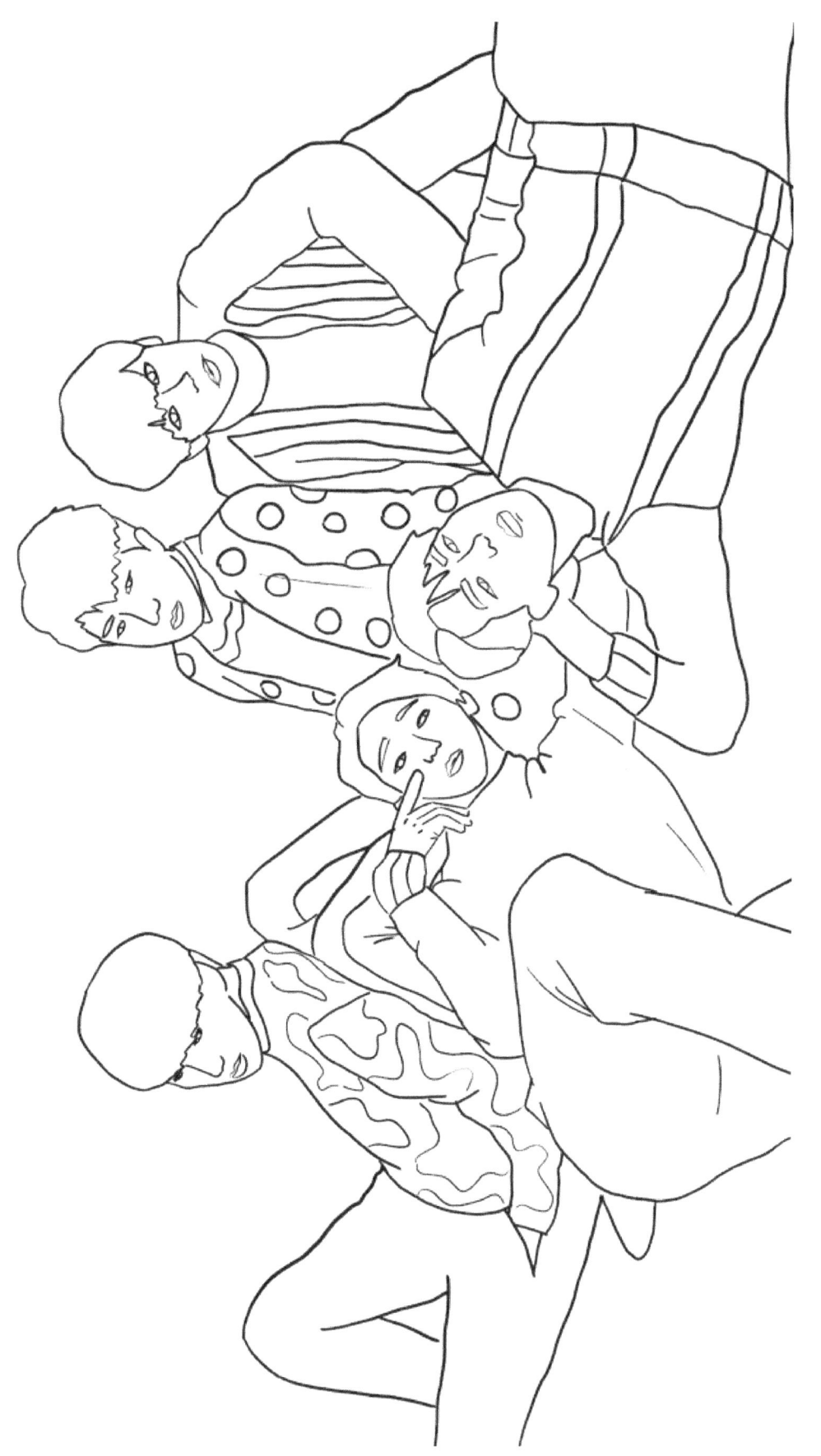

www.ingramcontent.com/pod-product-compliance
Lightning Source LLC
Chambersburg PA
CBHW081751170526
45167CB00009B/3999